VW CAMPER AND MICROBUS

Richard A. Copping

SHIRE PUBLICATIONS

First published in Great Britain in 2009 by Shire Publications Ltd, Midland House, West Way, Botley, Oxford OX2 0PH, United Kingdom.
443 Park Avenue South, New York, NY 10016, USA.

E-mail: shire@shirebooks.co.uk www.shirebooks.co.uk

A CIP catalogue record for this book is available from the British Library.

Shire Library no. 486 • ISBN-978 0 7478 0709 4

Richard A. Copping has asserted his right under the Copyright, Designs and Patents Act, 1988, to be identified as the author of this book.

Designed by Ken Vail Graphic Design, Cambridge, UK and typeset in Perpetua and Gill Sans.
Printed in China through Worldprint Ltd.

09 10 11 12 13 10 9 8 7 6 5 4 3 2 1

COVER IMAGE

The artwork might not be by Reuters but it does convey the late-1950s message about the passenger-carrying members of the Transporter line-up. Note the indicators and two-tier bumpers for the United States market.

TITLE PAGE IMAGE

The VW roundel, designed in the 1930s and modified for post-war use, was a prominent feature on both the first- and second-generation Transporter.

CONTENTS PAGE IMAGE

The Microbus Deluxe lost its two rear quarter-panel windows when the tailgate was enlarged, as this intriguing cut-out image indicates. Twenty-one windows were still sufficient, though!

ACKNOWLEDGEMENTS

The images on pages 8, 9, 10, and 22 were originally released by Volkswagen AG, while those on pages 36 and 60 were made available by Volkswagen UK. The services of the respective press offices are greatly appreciated. The photographs on pages 58 and 61 were taken by Carlee Castro and Steve Parsons. All other photographs belong to the author and all imagery is taken from the author's collection of Volkswagen sales literature.

CONTENTS

INTRODUCTION

BACK in the late 1980s few would have given a second glance to a Volkswagen Transporter, either the archaic split-screen model produced between 1950 and 1967, or its less than dynamic larger-windowed successor, on sale from August 1967 until the summer of 1979. Underpowered and cumbersome, they were – like any other redundant model – ever depreciating assets heading for the scrapyard as the years took their toll.

But for some time now, these old Volkswagens have not only achieved a status as sought-after icons of a bygone age, but also, as a direct consequence of such appeal, have been appreciating in value, a phenomenon so rare in the world of motor manufacturing as to be genuinely noteworthy. A concurrent spin-off of this popularity is the proliferation of china mugs bearing an image of these vehicles, salt and pepper sets created in their likeness, and prints capturing their retro feel, to mention but three examples. Meanwhile, coastal resorts are frequented by surfboard-bedecked, brightly painted and decorated VW Buses, a throwback to the days of the hippy. Formerly quiet campsites are the scene of conventions of elderly Volkswagens and their air-cooled clatter. Enthusiast gatherings attract massive numbers of owners and admirers; shows are packed to capacity or even outgrow their original venues.

The truth behind the cult of the Volkswagen Transporter is twofold: the happy smiling faces of the old Buses capture all that endears the 1950s and 1960s to modern man, while the growing trend towards back-to-basics outdoor enjoyment is nowhere better embodied than in an elderly and unsophisticated Camper van.

Volkswagen launched its first Transporters with little thought of a name, the model designation of Type 2 (the Beetle was the Type 1) being deemed sufficient in the haste to enter production. Fortunately, the situation was partially remedied through terms such as the 'Transporter' in Europe and the 'Bus' in the United States. Passenger-carrying versions in North America became 'VW Station Wagons' although the European formality of 'The Volkswagen Camper with Westfalia Deluxe Equipment', often seen in print,

Opposite: Photography and artwork used in brochures dating from the 1960s concentrated on living with a Transporter. The model shown is a Microbus.

Although Volkswagen did not build its own Camper until late 2004, much earlier vehicles have long been attributed with the term – owners enjoying an outdoor life to the full.

was rarely heard. The American or Australian designation of 'Campmobile' might sound contrived, as could the equally artificial term 'Vanagon', but at least owners could confirm their vehicle's origins through such names.

Throughout most of this book the Transporter is referred to by that name, which has gathered official status as the years have passed. But when we come to the period of customisation, lowering, rat-looks and hippy buses, deeply immersed in the realms of enthusiasm, the first-generation Transporter becomes the 'Splitty', while its successor is widely known as the 'Bay' – both nicknames being derived from the vehicle's windscreens.

Richard Copping, 2008

THE TRANSPORTER'S ORIGINS

THREE MEN played key parts in the story behind the creation of the Transporter. Perhaps surprisingly, the Beetle's originator, Ferdinand Porsche, was not one of them. His role ended with the saloon and its military siblings, these latter being built to assist the Nazi war effort. Hitler had been repeatedly obstructed by German motor manufacturers in his pre-war goal of delivering Porsche's 'people's car' to the masses and was determined that a factory dedicated to its production would be built. In 1945 the British took control of this heavily bombed and ownerless factory, known now as Wolfsburg. Porsche had fled and it was left to a British major, Ivan Hirst, to run the works, producing vehicles for transport-starved military personnel.

Renowned for his ingenuity in the face of crippling shortages, when British Army forklifts were withdrawn from Wolfsburg for use elsewhere, Hirst created a flatbed vehicle using the Beetle's chassis as its basis. A seat and primitive cab were positioned above the rear-mounted engine, and so the whole front end, amounting to some 75 per cent of the vehicle, could be allocated to easy load carrying. Named the 'Plattenwagen', this vehicle triggered the fertile imagination of the second player in the story of the Transporter's birth.

Variously described as extrovert, ebullient or opportunist, Dutchman Ben Pon was determined to secure a franchise to sell Beetles in his home country. Legend has it that Pon, temporarily commissioned a colonel in the Dutch Army, bedecked himself with phoney medals, hired a chauffeur, borrowed a Mercedes and made for Wolfsburg in high style. Hirst's superior officer, Charles Radclyffe, succumbed to Pon's charms, eliciting precious and hard-to-come-by steel from the Dutchman in return for cars. A relationship established, Pon was a regular visitor at Wolfsburg and it was on one such occasion that he encountered the Plattenwagen. Recalling the many pedal-powered delivery vehicles at home, Pon endeavoured to obtain street-legal specification for Hirst's petrol-powered invention, but without success. To the Dutch authorities the golden rule that the driver of any form of transport must sit at the front of the vehicle was sacrosanct.

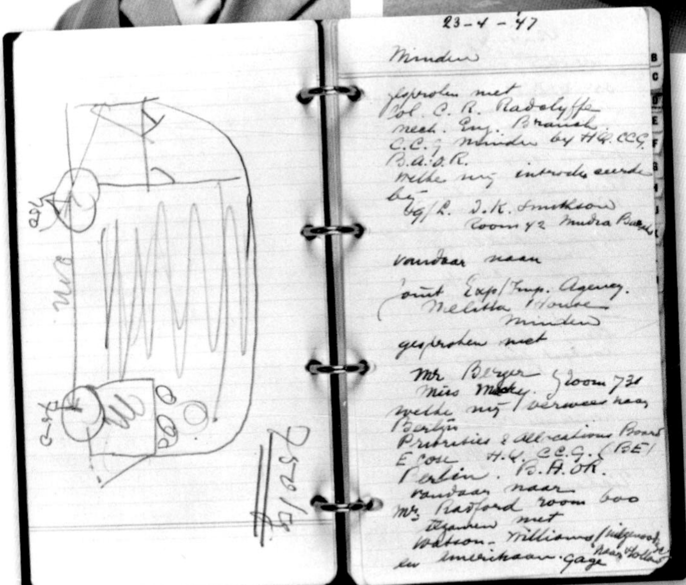

Top left:
Major Ivan Hirst, the British officer despatched to the Volkswagen factory in 1945 with no specific orders, and whose ingenuity in the face of extreme shortages made a major contribution to the operation's survival.

Top right:
The Plattenwagen, created by Ivan Hirst following the withdrawal of military vehicles, and the machine that led Ben Pon on the route that would culminate in his historic sketch.

Above:
Ben Pon's historic sketch of 23 April 1947 – a rudimentary affair that nevertheless bears a striking resemblance to the Transporter launched less than three years later.

Only temporarily discouraged, Pon met with Hirst on 23 April 1947 and promptly sketched a box-shaped vehicle that he envisaged would carry weights of around 750 kg, with its engine at the rear and cab up front, the driver sitting directly over the machine's steering wheels. Hirst was impressed with the effective simplicity of the design but was unable to progress the idea, as Radclyffe rightly prevented any distraction to Beetle production; resources simply would not allow it.

Heinz Nordhoff, the man who was to create a world-beater out of the still greatly flawed Beetle, joined Volkswagen in January 1948 as Director

General. British leadership had always been regarded as temporary. Nordhoff's career to date had culminated in promotion to the Opel board and the job of managing Europe's largest truck factory at Brandenburg. Denied work in the American zone of post-war Germany because of a minor award bestowed on him by the Nazis, Nordhoff's prospects looked bleak, until Hirst carried out initial interviews for the post of deputy to Hermann Munch, the German custodian at Wolfsburg. So much did Nordhoff impress that he succeeded Munch rather than working alongside him.

Pon's ideas came to the expert attention of Nordhoff and by the autumn of 1948 the decision had been taken to progress the project to full manufacture. On 20 November Nordhoff was presented with two options. Rejecting version A, with its flat and straight driver's cab, he selected choice B, a vehicle with a slightly raked front and without a projecting roof. Unfortunately, initial prototypes served only to demonstrate that a model based on a widened Beetle chassis was not robust enough. Weight placed in the load-carrying area resulted in the collapse of the Beetle's unmodified floor-pan. Tests begun on 11 March 1949 had to be halted on 5 April. Nordhoff was undeterred, and rebuilt prototypes included a near-unitised body, incorporating a distinctive chassis with longitudinal box sections and powerful outriggers for unbending support. Pressure from Nordhoff ensured

Heinz Nordhoff, Volkswagen's Director General from January 1948 until his death in April 1968. His experience and determination brought the Transporter from concept to reality in record time.

The first of the line, the Delivery Van, as it was revealed to the world's press in 1949. (Volkswagen AG)

that tests recommenced in May, and 12,000 kilometres driven on the worst of German roads without mishap was sufficient to convince him that a production starting date could be set. On 19 May 1949 this was duly announced as 1 November 1949, or at worst as 1 December of the same year. So the pressure was on to start delivery of the new Volkswagen at the beginning of 1950.

While many might well have assumed that activity would have been restricted to a basic van, this was clearly never Nordhoff's intention. On 15 August it was revealed that in addition to the Delivery Van, a Pick-up, an eight-seat minibus and a vehicle suitable for use by the ambulance service were to be ready in no more than two months. Nordhoff demanded many changes to the specification, continually bombarding his technical director, Alfred Haesner, with ideas to increase potential sales. The prototypes, consisting of two Delivery vans, a Microbus and an aptly named 'Kombi', were sufficiently advanced by 12 November to be presented to the press.

Nordhoff sold the new vehicle's advantages to the full, describing it in these words: 'As our car is without compromise, so will our Transporter be without compromise. This is why we did not start from an available chassis but from the cargo space. This is the clean, no compromise principle of our Transporter. With this van and only this van, the cargo space lies exactly between the axles. In front sits the driver and in the back is the same weight due to the engine and the fuel tank. That is the best compromise ... We would have put the engine in the front without hesitation if this had been a better solution ... However, the famous "cab above the engine" gave such horrendous handling characteristics when loaded that we never even considered it. You can tell from the state of the roadside trees in the entire British Zone how the lorries of the English Army, which have been built according to this principle, handle when they are unladen.'

His promotional task successfully accomplished, Nordhoff ensured feverish activity so that the first Delivery Vans rolled off the assembly line in February 1950. Although these were reserved as test vehicles for Wolfsburg's most important customers, the Transporter went on sale officially in March, having made its public debut at the Geneva Motor Show. Production at a rate of ten vehicles per day started on 10 March.

SPECIFICATION GUIDE

Although the Transporter appeared to be a much larger vehicle than the Beetle, this was not the case, for the two vehicles shared a wheelbase of 2,400 mm. However, the front track for the commercial was 1,356 mm, compared to 1,290 mm for the car, and a similar disparity was evident at the rear as the commercial measured 1,360 mm compared to the car's 1,250 mm. The difference in the overall length of the two Volkswagens amounted to just 50 mm, the Transporter totalling 4,100 mm and the Beetle 4,050 mm. In breadth there was an understandable size variation in favour of the Transporter at 1,660 mm compared to the car's 1,540 mm, while, to achieve maximum storage capacity, the height of the commercial vehicle at 1,540 mm towered over that of the saloon at 1,500 mm.

Considering that the Transporter was expected to convey loads of up to 750 kg, it might be thought unrealistic for it to share the Beetle's 25 PS (metric horsepower or Pferdestärke) engine, but there was no other option available to an operation with very few financial reserves. The 1,131cc air-cooled flat-four unit, with a bore and stroke of 75mm by 64 mm, and a compression ratio of 5.8:1, when mated to the weight of the Splitty offered a top speed of 92 km/h unladen and 85 km/h when fully loaded. Hence, the now traditional 0–100 km/h figure beloved of motoring journalists was entirely academic! Concerned for the long term, Nordhoff and his team suggested a top speed of 80 km/h and fixed a sticker to the vehicle's windscreen warning of this stipulation. As a bonus, to negate the worst effects on performance caused by even the slightest incline, reduction gears in the

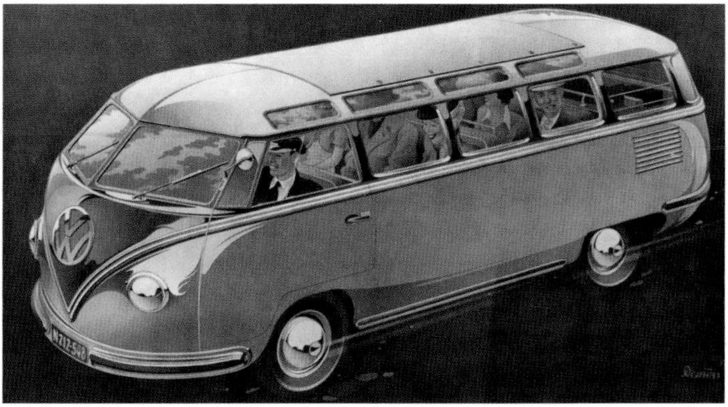

The top of the range Microbus Deluxe featured a wealth of additional brightwork and, even more importantly, a specification that included twenty-three windows.

rear wheel hubs, an innovation of Porsche's, previously seen in use on the all-terrain Kübelwagen, were incorporated into the design.

In appearance, the earliest Transporters differed somewhat from those produced in later years. The largest panel was that for the roof, as it was made out of a single piece of metal. One means of detecting a van built before March 1955 has always been to check for a distinctive swage line at the front of the roof that lined up directly with the division between the two panes forming the windscreen. After that date, the swage line disappeared with the installation of a more effective ventilation system, which in itself was cause for elements of redesign at the vehicle's front end.

The partially double-skinned panel with Y-shaped swage lines below the windscreen more than any other factor characterised the Transporter's appearance, seeming almost to bestow feelings of happiness on it. Early models lacked the indicators that would later perch almost precariously

Throughout the 1950s Volkswagen relied heavily on the artwork of Bernd Reuters to promote each variant on the Transporter theme. This artwork highlights two features of a pre-1955 Transporter: the considerable size of its engine compartment lid, and the absence of a metal peak between the windscreen and the roof panel.

above and to the right and left respectively of the headlamp pods, relying instead on semaphores perilously placed behind the driver and passenger windows.

Opening quarter-lights, a device the Beetle lacked until October 1952, in early guise were adjusted by means of a piano-hinge type of arrangement, a feature that unfortunately prevented an adequate flow of air entering the cab.

Until April 1951 all Transporters lacked any form of rear window, although an exceptionally tiny one could be specified as an optional extra at additional cost. Before November 1950 a massive VW roundel sat where the window would have been, while before March 1953 no option in the range was equipped with any form of rear bumper.

However, there was one item above all others that characterised early models, apart from the Pick-up and the much less frequently seen Ambulance. This was the vehicle's massive engine lid. Indeed, so large was the cover that Transporters built before March 1955 (when the design changed) are collectively referred to as 'Barn Door' vehicles! Although access to the engine was incredibly easy, as one might imagine, the design lacked convenient entry to the loading or passenger-carrying space, this being available only via the double opening side doors. In addition to the engine, the cavernous compartment contained the vehicle's fuel tank and filler cap, making it necessary to open the lid every time refuelling was needed. There was plenty of room for the spare wheel, which at first sat vertically but by 1951 had its own shelf above the engine, on which it might be placed horizontally.

To enthusiasts Transporters built before March 1955 are known as 'Barn Door' models, because of the extraordinarily large lid to the engine compartment.

The vehicle sat on 16-inch wheels, fitted with skinny $5^1/_2$ by 16-inch cross-ply tyres and was equipped with nothing more subtle than a crash-box until March 1953 (when synchromesh became standard on all but first gear), but, unlike the Beetle, it was brought to a halt with hydraulic brakes from the beginning.

VIEWEG
BH 202-377

MODEL VARIATIONS

PROTOTYPE production indicated that a single model of Transporter was never Nordhoff's master plan. He wanted a range of bodies, utilising the same basic construction, in order to maximise potential sales, and the individual model production figures achieved in the early years provided ample evidence to vindicate his approach.

Soon after the Delivery Van's official launch on 9 March 1950 came those of the Kombi on 16 May and the Microbus on 22 May. Both additions were of vital importance, the former inspiring the revolutionary concept that became the Camper, the latter being widely acknowledged as a genuine forerunner of the multifarious people-carriers so commonplace today. Just over a year later, on 1 June 1951, two further tweaks of the passenger-carrying theme emerged: a Microbus with a canvas slide-back roof; and a Deluxe version with both sunroof and a multitude of windows extending into both the roof section and the rear quarter panels of the vehicle. This latter version, more than any other, indicated that Nordhoff and his team were starting to amass sufficient capital to be able to go beyond the basics. On 13 December of the same year an Ambulance was added to the list of options, a specialist vehicle that surely offered a signal that with the Transporter just about anything was possible. A little over eight months later, a vehicle that was much more expensive to create, the Pick-up, with new roof and cab panels plus a heavily re-engineered engine compartment, was offered.

Although their arrival was still some years in the future, it is worth mentioning the versatile Double Cab Pick-up of late 1958 vintage, particularly popular in the United States, and the High Roof Delivery Van – convenient for the clothing trade – which appeared in September 1961. These additions to the core range lead directly to what were referred to as *Sonderausführungen*, or special models: by 1961 Volkswagen was able to list 131 of these variations on the Transporter theme.

Although some of the specials were built by Volkswagen, by far the greater proportion were prepared by *Karosserien*, or coachworks, for which Germany was renowned. (Indeed, the Cabriolet version of the Beetle was not

Opposite:
These early images appear to be intended to demonstrate that the Microbus Deluxe came with a fold-back canvas sunroof as standard.

Another fine example of Reuters's artwork. Note the exaggerated length of the van, and the seemingly tiny people in the cab.

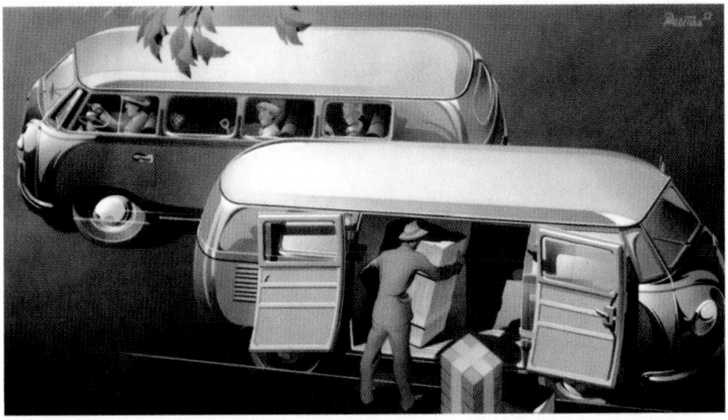

One minute the Kombi could act as a Delivery Van, the next as a people-carrier – the inspiration behind the first removable camping kits.

The VW Ambulance came after the Microbus Deluxe as the next main model in the sequence. With its opening rear hatch designed to accommodate a stretcher, it was ahead of its time.

manufactured at Wolfsburg but was put into the skilled hands of the Karmann Karosserie based in Osnabrück.) One firm, Westfalia, although not strictly a coachbuilder, would triumph above all others in a partnership with Volkswagen based on the first-generation Transporter. Models produced ranged from a mobile shop and a refrigerated meat van, to a hydraulic tipper truck and a catering van.

Many a Delivery Van left the factory coated with nothing more than primer, as Volkswagen's marketing department convinced owners of the merits of having the new vehicle finished in their company's livery, with all the advertising advantages such a strategy could offer. In terms of sales percentages compared to total production, the workhorse Delivery Van remained by far the most popular option throughout the seventeen years of the first-generation Transporter's manufacture. In 1954, an early year, but one in which most of the main variants were available, out of a total production figure of 40,119, Delivery Vans accounted for 36.3 per cent, with the Kombi at 22 per cent proving to be the second most popular. The top of the range Microbus Deluxe sold no more than 1,937 vehicles, or a little under 5 per cent of the whole.

In terms of survivors, however, the number of Delivery Vans, and particularly Pick-ups, might well be counted on the hands of a very few people, this being entirely due to their valuable role in working life. The people-carriers fared better, and it is to these models that our attention is now turned. Of the three options, the cheapest, yet most versatile, was the Kombi. Around 1956 in the United States a Kombi would have cost $2,130 (making it $200 more expensive than a Delivery Van). A Microbus of the

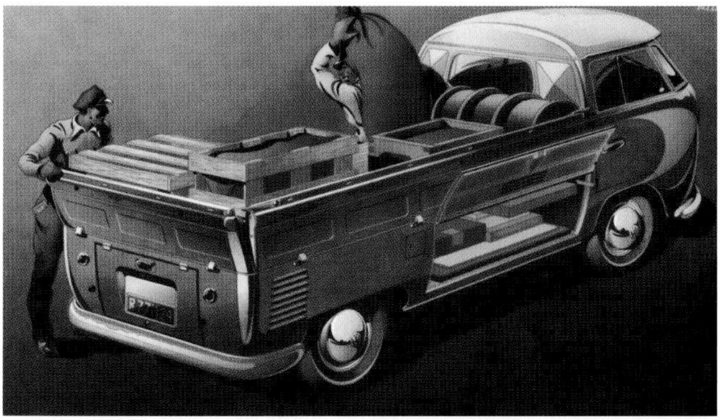

The Pick-up made its debut in 1952 – a useful addition to the range, but one that required significant investment on the part of Volkswagen to initiate.

The Microbus is well described as the forerunner of present-day people-carriers, although Reuters's artwork makes it look more spacious than it really was.

With the Microbus, Volkswagen clearly intended to market an outdoor, 'away from it all' lifestyle
.

same vintage could be purchased for $2,230, but its Deluxe sibling commanded a price of $2,685.

The German term 'Kombi' was sufficiently descriptive for it to be adopted across the many countries that would eventually come to sell it. The vehicle was undoubtedly a primitive affair, but equally revolutionary in its concept. It was essentially a Delivery Van with side windows and a surplus of seats. Its interior, other than the cab area, consisted of nothing more than painted metal. Its flexibility ensured its success, as either one or both rear bench seats could be easily removed simply by unscrewing a series of wingnuts. Larger loads could be accommodated by removing all the seats, and smaller ones by taking out just one bench. Some owners tended to use the vehicle as a van during the week and transform it into passenger transport for family enjoyment at weekends. Such usage triggered further thoughts, with which the name Westfalia would be associated.

The Kleinbus, or Microbus, initially seated seven persons in addition to the driver. It was carefully trimmed with colour co-ordinated leatherette. While by today's standards the vehicle would have appeared very basic, in its day it deserved its American attribution of 'Station Wagon', a widely used term that had little to do with the American 'truck' and equated more closely with the British description of such vehicles as estate cars, or the German expression 'Variant'. A brochure even made reference to the word 'comfort'. Before long, although not initially, the Microbus could be specified with a fold-back canvas sunroof, manufactured for Volkswagen by the firm of Golde.

The top of the range model, the Kleinbus Sonderausführung, or Microbus Deluxe, was a remarkable vehicle in its day – light, airy, and particularly well appointed with the most tasteful of furnishings – and featured the fold-back canvas sunroof as standard. With this open, all eight potential passengers, plus the driver, who according to the sales patter was often deemed to be a chauffeur, would have benefited from nearly all the advantages of cabriolet motoring, but it was with its abundance of windows that the top model scored. Early Microbus Deluxe vehicles are known by enthusiasts as 'twenty-three-window buses'. Compared to both the lowly Kombi and the less magnificent Microbus, the top model featured an extra window down each flank, while the upper rear quarter panels were also glazed. Finally, what Volkswagen referred to in one sales brochure as 'Plexiglass lateral deck windows' but might most aptly be described as roof-lights – totalling eight in number, and consisting of four slender rectangular panes down each side – ensured that, even on the dullest of days, passengers enjoyed plenty of daylight. Curved glass was both difficult and expensive to manufacture at the time, so Volkswagen used Plexiglass, a material similar in nature to Perspex, to glaze these rounded windows.

Before March 1955 the Microbus Deluxe was the only model in the range to feature a full-length dashboard, the others relying on a single binnacle housing the simple instrument panel. Such luxury made room to house a clock as standard, while a blanking plan was ready built in should an owner decide to add a radio to the package. The Microbus Deluxe also looked its part thanks to additional brightwork trim, most notably in the form of double strips tracing the swage lines on both the vehicle's sides and the Y-shaped contours of its front. The rearmost windows were safeguarded with chromed bars, often referred to now as 'jail bars'. Even the VW roundel on the front of the vehicle was enhanced, having chrome rather than a painted finish.

All Kombis left the factory either finished in a single paint colour, or in primer ready for customising by the vehicle's first owner. While both the Microbus and the Microbus Deluxe could be specified in a single colour, the option being Stone Grey before the end of February 1955 and Sand Grey for a year or two afterwards, most owners selected two-tone finishes. The upper body colour of the Microbus before March 1955 would have been Brown Beige and the lower panels a contrasting Light Beige. The Deluxe model displayed a combination of Chestnut Brown over Sealing Wax Red paintwork.

TRANSPORTER VARIANTS

WITH a production run spanning seventeen years, inevitably a Transporter manufactured in 1967 differed considerably from the models that had rolled off the assembly line in 1950. Heinz Nordhoff, Volkswagen's Director General throughout the period, was a great advocate of a process of continual improvement, which he extended to all models in the range and most noticeably to the Beetle. Consequently, many were shocked to learn as the 1960s progressed that a replacement for the much-loved and still highly successful first-generation Transporter might even be countenanced, let alone effected, so far was this a diversion from the norm.

At the end of 1953 the original 1,131cc 25 PS engine was replaced by a new 1,192cc unit with 30 PS available at 3,400 rpm. Although the boost appears paltry today, with only a small increase in the vehicle's top speed, nevertheless the additional 5 PS offered distinct advantages at the lower end of the speed range, torque having increased from 67 Nm (newton metres) at 2,000 rpm to 76 Nm at 2,000 rpm, and was widely welcomed.

The next major development came in early March 1955 when the design of the vehicle was fundamentally revised. The crease line at the front end of the roof disappeared, to be replaced by a smooth panel with a distinct peaked overhang. This contained intakes for much improved cab and interior ventilation, controllable via handles attached to an interior roof-mounted collection and distribution box. All models benefited from a full-length dashboard instead of a single control binnacle, the only Transporter to have been so equipped previously being the Microbus Deluxe. Apart from the improvement in looks this afforded, a revised arrangement of heater outlets, made possible by such a redesign, ensured more effective defrosting and warm-air circulation.

That the spare wheel now sat behind the front bench seat, necessitating a revision to the division between the cab and the load- or passenger-carrying area in the form of protruding metalwork to accommodate its bulk, was the result of drastic activity at the vehicle's rear. Swept away were the massive engine-compartment lid and the cavernous compartment set aside to house

Opposite:
In the last days of the first generation of Transporters, Volkswagen chose to illustrate sales literature with a line-up of the most popular models in the range.

Volkswagen's post-1955 cab ventilation system demanded a redesign of the roof panel, creating a peak to house air-intake panels.

the engine. With this area drastically reduced in size without making it difficult to work on the engine, it was possible to create a second opening lid in addition to the new and much smaller one that gave access for servicing. The new lid gave direct access to a flat platform set aside for luggage, or additional boxes in the case of the Delivery Van. An external fuel cap made filling up far more convenient, while the reduction of the sizes of the wheels from

This style of indicator, introduced to the United States market in 1955 and to the rest of the world in 1960, is usually referred to as the bullet style.

These press images of the post-March 1955 Microbus Deluxe and Microbus both illustrate clearly the new metal peak.

A fine example of Bernd Reuters's work – exaggerated lines, tiny out-of-scale people giving an impression of roominess, brush lines to imply pace of movement, and a vast sunroof: hardly truthful, but nowadays highly collectable!

16 inches to 15 inches, and the fitting of wider tyres, helped to ensure a more modern feel.

Antiquated semaphore indicators were abolished for American and Canadian purchasers from April 1955, their replacements being bullet-style indicators neatly attached to the front panel. This particular upgrade had been forced on Volkswagen by impending legislation in the United States, and European owners had to wait until June 1960 for such an improvement.

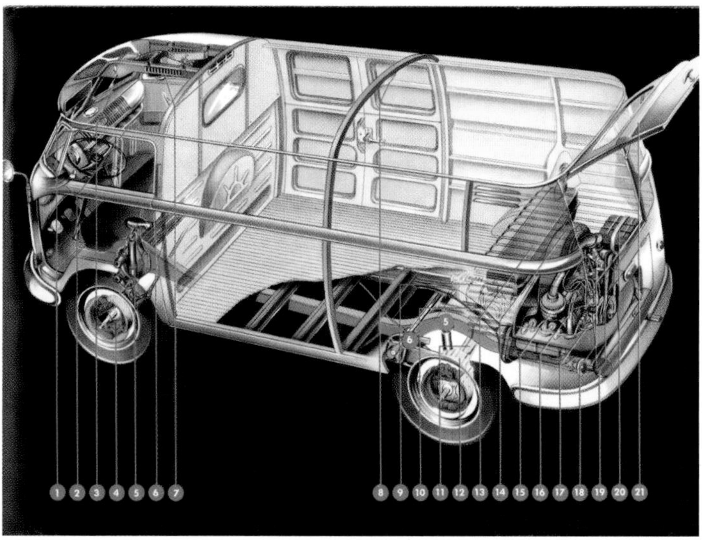

The cutaway drawing of a post-March 1955 vehicle illustrates the cab ventilation system, the full-length dashboard, the pressing behind the cab seat to make room for the spare wheel, the rear loading hatch, and the smaller engine lid.

From August 1955, Transporters destined for the North American market were fitted with bullet-style front indicators, while from August 1958 they also featured two-tier bumpers. The model depicted is a Kombi, to which seats could be added.

Similarly, in August 1958, American-bound vehicles were fitted with two-tier bumpers consisting of sturdy lower blades, large overriders, and more delicate upper bars that were soon endearingly likened to towel rails. This attractive development led many a European purchaser to specify such an accessory.

In May 1959 a sturdier version of the already highly reliable 30 PS engine, with a slightly higher compression ratio, was introduced, although its lifespan was short, for in June 1960 an upgrade in even the most humble Transporter's power was announced. This came in the form of a new 34 PS

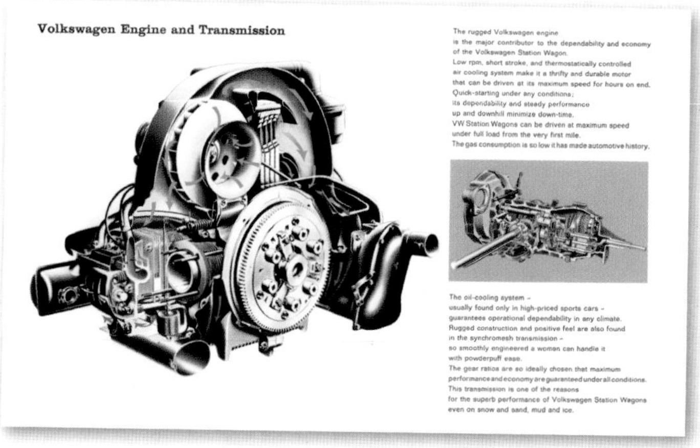

Volkswagen Engine and Transmission

The rugged Volkswagen engine
is the major contributor to the dependability and economy
of the Volkswagen Station Wagon.
Low rpm, short stroke, and thermostatically controlled
air cooling system make it a thrifty and durable motor
that can be driven at its maximum speed for hours on end.
Quick-starting under any conditions;
its dependability and steady performance
up and downhill minimize down-time.
VW Station Wagons can be driven at maximum speed
under full load from the very first mile.
The gas consumption is so low it has made automotive history.

The oil-cooling system –
usually found only in high-priced sports cars –
guarantees operational dependability in any climate.
Rugged construction and positive feel are also found
in the synchromesh transmission –
so smoothly engineered a woman can handle it
with powderpuff ease.
The gear ratios are so ideally chosen that maximum
performance and economy are guaranteed under all conditions.
This transmission is one of the reasons
for the superb performance of Volkswagen Station Wagons
even on snow and sand, mud and ice.

June 1960 brought not only a significant engine upgrade, but also a changing style in sales literature. This was one of the last occasions when line drawings would be employed.

engine, with a raised compression ratio of 7.0:1, plus a 28 PICT carburettor. Optimum power was achieved at 3,600 rpm, while maximum torque of 82 Nm was realised at 2,000 rpm. Finally, the ratio of the reduction gears in the axle hubs was changed from 1.4:1 to 1.39:1. As when the 30 PS engine replaced the 25 PS engine nearly seven years earlier, there was little change in terms of the vehicle's top speed but, again as previously, the 'new' Transporter felt much livelier with better acceleration through the gears.

New and larger rear lights, a further style of front indicator lamp for the United States market and a revised and larger housing for the spare wheel (necessitated by the introduction of a separate driver's seat instead of the single cab bench of old) all appeared between the arrival of the 34 PS engine and that of a 1,493cc, 42 PS power unit, introduced, at least for the American market, at the start of 1963. The lesser-powered 1200 remained optional for

From 1961 in the United States, and 1963 in Europe, Transporters were fitted with larger front indicators, as illustrated on this Microbus (top). This style of indicator (above) was known as the 'fish-eye flasher' to enthusiasts.

The arrival of the 1500 engine in 1963 was presented to potential purchasers in a very different way from previous such developments. Notice the larger rear light cluster, an introduction dating from 1961.

Why make the VW Commercial's rear door and window even bigger?
Large practical wing doors are nothing new as far as the VW Commercial's concerned. (There is more about this in our big catalogue.) In addition to this, however, you'll discover that VW Commercials have a door in the rear (very practical it is too). We've just made the rear door and the window bigger than ever. What is the reason?
A larger door means that larger items can be carried in and out. The larger it is the easier — and quicker — you do the job of loading (or unloading).
The wider rear window helps you to see better what's going on behind. This makes it easier to park in heavy traffic, than it was before. You may have a question . . . How much more does a VW Commercial cost now that we've enlarged both the rear door and rear window? For us it means more work, more expense. It does not cost you a penny more, however. In turn that means the VW Commercial is now even more of a bargain.

Promoting the larger tailgate and rear window of August 1963 in the Doyle Dane Bernbach house style – simple but highly effective!

other markets from March of the same year, but its sales decreased, resulting in its deletion from the range in October 1965. In reality the 1500 was little more than a bored-out 1200. An increased bore and stroke of 83 mm and 69 mm respectively, plus a further increase in compression to 7.5:1, resulted in an 8 PS increase in power at 3,800 rpm. Of most interest to those purchasing a Delivery Van, a Pick-up or conceivably a Kombi, the vehicle's payload went up from 750 kg to 1,000 kg. Nordhoff's cautionary top speed was now quoted at 105 km/h, but when it was realised that owners were driving at least 16 km/h in excess of such a figure the Hanover factory fitted a carburettor throttle governor. Fortunately, the arrival of a more efficient carburettor in the shape of the 28 PICT 1 in August 1965, coupled to an increase in the size of the inlet and outlet valve diameters, allowed the engine to breathe more easily. The PS rating went up slightly to 44 PS, a figure achieved at 4,000 rpm.

Somewhat belatedly, in August 1963, the Transporter's tailgate was increased in size, the change being linked with a much-needed enlargement of the rear window. Manoeuvring any of the variants became considerably easier thanks to the increased visibility, although there was a casualty in the upgrade, at least in terms of aesthetics, in that the twenty-three-window Microbus Deluxe lost its curved rear quarter panes of glass, becoming a mere twenty-one-window vehicle in the process! For the second time in the vehicle's history, the wheels were reduced in size, on this occasion the old 15-inch ones being replaced by 14-inch versions.

A final significant change occurred in the summer of 1966 when the rather antiquated 6-volt electrical arrangement was replaced by an altogether more acceptable 12-volt system. For the American market dual circuit braking and reversing lights became standard.

SALES PERFORMANCE AND OVERSEAS MARKETS

More than 1,833,000 Transporters were built between February 1950 and the last days of July 1967. While this might appear trifling in comparison to the venerable Beetle, which in 1965 alone accounted for over one million sales, the vehicle was a valuable asset to Volkswagen and one of which it could rightly be proud. Suitably garlanded models were rolled off the assembly line to the accompaniment of speeches by either Nordhoff or one of his lieutenants as each notable production figure was successfully passed. The 100,000th Transporter was produced on 9 October 1954, the 500,000th on 25 August 1959, and the million figure was achieved on 20 September 1962.

From the ten vehicles per day produced in 1950, the number had climbed to 170 in 1954, a figure that Wolfsburg, even with overtime, found difficult to cope with because of the relentless demand for Beetles. The lack of available labour to meet demands for the Transporter, which now realistically required a daily production rate of at least double what was practical, led Nordhoff to the decision that a new factory should be built at Hanover – an ideal location in terms of its network of roads, rail links and access to the sea but, above all else, perfect in terms of the available workforce on which Volkswagen could call. The decision was made in January 1955, a site had been acquired by February, and construction commenced the following month. On 9 March 1956, a Pick-up was the first vehicle to leave the new assembly line, one of 247 Transporters to be built every day. In 1960 Nordhoff advised dealers and distributors that the factory produced '530 a day' and that he was 'certain that even this was not enough!' Towards the end of first-generation production, daily output was above eight hundred vehicles.

The factory employed 23,000 workers by this time and had also taken over Volkswagen's engine-building programme.

1958 was the last year in which fewer than 100,000 Transporters were produced in a twelve-month period at Hanover, while the peak came in 1964 when 187,947 left the factory. Nordhoff had been determined that the Beetle would be exported to countries throughout the world and, thanks to its ground-breaking attributes, the commercial vehicle and its people-carrying variants tended to follow.

The story of how the Beetle finally broke into the American market is reasonably well known, as is Nordhoff's rugged determination to succeed, however long it took. Transporter exports to America, like those of the Beetle, were insignificant before 1954, when 827 such vehicles made their way across the Atlantic. From this modest beginning, the numbers of Transporters finding their way into American showrooms increased annually to a figure of 32,133 in 1959. The best year was 1966, when over 40,000 models of one description or another were exported.

The official invasion of Britain by Volkswagen began in 1953. Few Beetles were sold and the fledgling operation recorded a significant loss. By 1955, 1,054 Transporter imports were supplementing Beetle sales, to the benefit of all concerned. The new decade brought a remarkable upturn in business, with a leap to 3,029 Transporters imported in twelve months, a pattern that would remain more or less intact until the end of first-generation Transporter production.

While Nordhoff was content to export to his European neighbours and to markets such as those already mentioned, if an opportunity arose to achieve more it was duly taken. Between 1950 and 1954, 831 Transporters were despatched to Brazil, but with effect from March 1953 'Volkswagen do Brasil SA' started assembling 'completely knocked-down' (CKD) kits supplied by Wolfsburg. Although no more than five Transporters per day were assembled, it was a start, and by 1957, following a factory move and an increase in Brazilian content to close on 50 per cent of the total, a boom was developing. On 28 December 1960 the 500,000th Brazilian-built Transporter rolled off the assembly line. By this time the factory possessed its own fully equipped pressing facility. During the 1960s annual production of Kombis, as both the first- and second-generation Transporters of any shape or form were known in Brazil, fluctuated between a low of 12,400 Kombis in 1964 and a high of 15,000 in 1966.

Australia received its first Transporter imports in 1953 and by June of the following year CKD assembly had started. In 1958 Volkswagen (Australasia) was formed, with 51 per cent of its shareholding belonging to the Volkswagenwerk back in Germany. By 1961 the company's factory at Clayton, virtually a suburb of Melbourne, had its own body shop, where it could press even the largest panel, the roof section, of the Transporter. In 1964 Volkswagen AG bought out the other interested parties on its road to full manufacture in Australia. Transporters built in Australia differed from their European counterparts, one of the most notable distinctions being first a single row of air vents above the swage line, and later a double row, both of which were designed to help the engine in the exceptionally dry and dusty climate. In a further deviation from the practices of the parent company, by 1961 local private converters were happily copying Westfalia's designs to create their own Campers – an extremely popular vehicle in such a country.

MARKETING THE TRANSPORTER

For many years now enthusiasts have collected the sales brochures produced by Volkswagen in the 1950s to promote the Beetle, the first-generation Transporter and the sporty-looking Karmann Ghia. Although the main device used – exquisite artwork – was far from unique to Wolfsburg, the skills of the key artist employed for the purpose, Bernd Reuters, were without equal. Reuters improved the looks of the vehicles by elongating the lines and exaggerating the curves. He added subtle speed streaks, while adjusting the size of the driver and passengers in relation to the vehicle, resulting in the early Transporter appearing roomier than it really was. The Delivery Van appeared to carry more than it was ever designed to, while the Microbus was truly palatial in its accommodation. Despite such overstatements of the Transporter's attributes, Reuters's drawings accurately depicted each model's

Photography, as well as line drawings, was used in the 1950s and some pictures showed that great care had been taken in the composition. Accompanying text tended to be rather turgid.

Reuters was commissioned to promote the new look of the Transporter after its 1955 revamp. The vehicle's new peaked front is apparent, but the aesthetics of the design are lost in this piece of exaggeration.

facets, to such an extent that, should a feature be added or revised part way into the production run, the artist would immediately adjust his drawing accordingly. On a larger scale, when the peaked front was introduced in March 1955, Reuters was commissioned to promote the new look and set about producing hill-climbing Transporters with split screens facing upwards to show off the peak to perfection. Reuters's undoubted skill served Volkswagen well for the best part of a decade.

Carl Hahn, originally Nordhoff's personal assistant, and a future Director General of Volkswagen, was appointed head of Volkswagen in the United States in 1959. Conscious that the Detroit-based car manufacturers were eagerly looking to produce their own cars to combat the rising challenge set by the

The Larger Volkswagen for Large Families and Small Parties
Volkswagen Station Wagon
and De Luxe Station Wagon

The style was changing as the 1950s drew to a close, although artwork still predominated. Volkswagen's fellow manufacturers were following similar lines – at least for the moment.

Above left:
No flattery, no unusual angles and, in many instances, no background. One clear message per advertisement – in this case, the Transporter looking like a bus, but with all the merits of a car.

Above right:
One simple message again, courtesy of Doyle Dane Bernbach. They both carry passengers – one carries more than the other.

Beetle, Hahn adopted a policy that Nordhoff would have been unlikely to countenance. Instead of letting the Beetle and the Transporter sell themselves through their proven attributes, Hahn wanted an aggressive marketing campaign that openly promoted both vehicles to additional buyers. After much deliberation he chose a firm with little more than ten years' experience behind it to promote the Beetle. This was the Doyle Dane Bernbach agency, known in the business simply as DDB. Such was their innovative approach that within twelve months Hahn had replaced Fuller, Smith & Ross, his choice to promote the vehicle Americans knew as the Bus or Station Wagon, with DDB. Realistic, often stark images replaced flattering artwork; self-congratulatory and often dull text was dismissed in favour of self-deprecating, but pithy and brutally honest words. Such an approach was unprecedented and, while it took the world of advertising by storm, it also did no harm to Volkswagen sales as both the Beetle and the ubiquitous Transporter became fashionable vehicles that any member of society had to be seen driving. DDB's influence spread rapidly across Volkswagen's empire and justifiably so.

Above:
The skill of a DDB advertisement was not just in the image. The copy was the envy of motor manufacturers the world over – one story again: how much room there was in the Microbus Deluxe.

Above right:
Such was the skill of the photographer and the recognition of the brand that it was not necessary to depict a whole vehicle, or to give this brochure cover a title.

'Why your next employee should be a Volkswagen' is the statement on a brochure cover – a reason being that 'they work for less': this style of advertising has more to it than retro appeal.

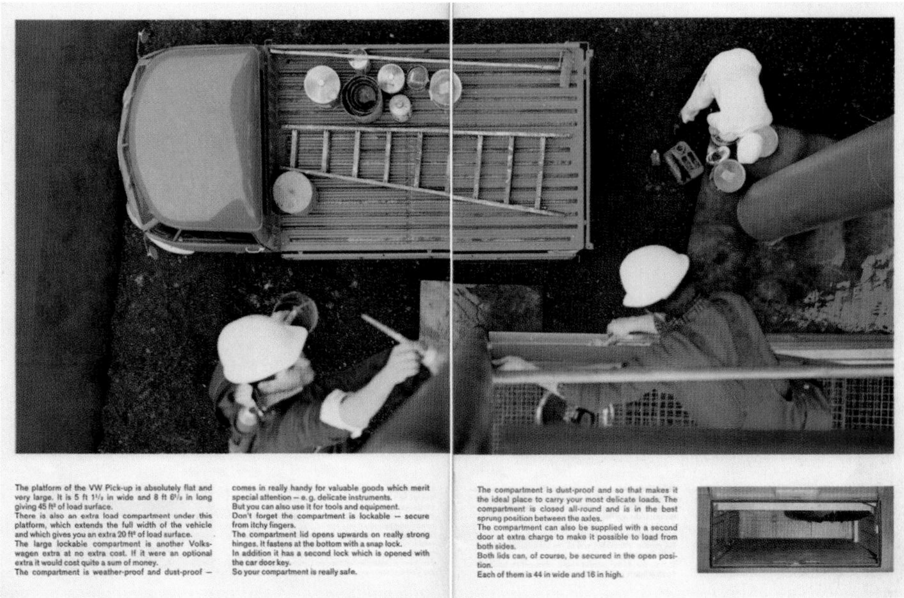

The platform of the VW Pick-up is absolutely flat and very large. It is 5 ft 1½ in wide and 8 ft 6½ in long giving 45 ft² of load surface.
There is also an extra load compartment under this platform, which extends the full width of the vehicle and which gives you an extra 20 ft² of load surface.
The large lockable compartment is another Volkswagen extra at no extra cost. If it were an optional extra it would cost quite a sum of money.
The compartment is weather-proof and dust-proof – comes in really handy for valuable goods which merit special attention – e.g. delicate instruments.
But you can also use it for tools and equipment.
Don't forget the compartment is lockable – secure from itchy fingers.
The compartment lid opens upwards on really strong hinges. It fastens at the bottom with a snap lock.
In addition it has a second lock which is opened with the car door key.
So your compartment is really safe.
The compartment is dust-proof and so that makes it the ideal place to carry your most delicate loads. The compartment is closed all-round and is in the best sprung position between the axles.
The compartment can also be supplied with a second door at extra charge to make it possible to load from both sides.
Both lids can, of course, be secured in the open position.
Each of them is 44 in wide and 16 in high.

Above:
Some might say that brochures were too clever in the mid 1960s, but demonstrating the size of the flat bed on a Pick-up was essential.

Getaway car!
Our getaway car is a Volkswagen Campmobile. It's sort of a three-room house on wheels. There's a living room. Or dining room. Or bedroom. (Depending on how you set it up.) It's a mountain retreat. A private cabana. A cottage on the lake. (Depending on where you want to go.)
And it's nice going in a VW Campmobile. No hotel, motel, resort or restaurant bills. No reservations, packing, or tipping porters. It's self-sufficient. Great for people who'd rather look at scenery than at No Vacancy signs. Great, too, for quietly stealing away. (People can't visit you if they can't find you.)
Any Standard Station Wagon, Kombi or Panel Truck we make can be a Campmobile. It's just a matter of getting one of our Campmobile Kits. For super de luxe living get our Super De Luxe Kit. Beds for four big people and two little people. Icebox. Stove. Running water Dinette. Shower And john.
There's even an upstairs.
If you prefer light housekeeping, get our Basic Kit. (See next page.) That way you can add things as you go along. Like a two-burner stove. Or luggage rack.
The nice thing about any of our Campmobiles is that when you return home (if you ever do), it will happily settle down and become itself again. All you have to do is remove the main components. (Once installed, they can be quickly taken out or put back in.) And you have a station wagon or delivery truck again.
Suggestion: Take your next vacation in a Campmobile. It's a very moving experience.

Campers sold in the United States in the 1960s followed in the style of the Station Wagons and commercial vehicles.

The VW Microbus L

With 212 cu. ft. inside.
35 cu. ft. of which is luggage space.

SECOND-GENERATION TRANSPORTERS

FIRST-GENERATION Transporter production came to an end in July 1967, an all-new model being offered from August of the same year. Nordhoff, who was by now well past the customary retirement age, had given his approval for the development of a second-generation Microbus and commercial vehicle at the end of 1964, confounding those who insisted that he was incapable of retiring outdated models. The Director General, who was no longer in the best of health, would live to see the two-millionth such vehicle roll off the assembly line in February 1968 – a Microbus L finished in Titian Red, which was donated to the charity Aktion Sorgenkind – but less than two months later Heinz Nordhoff died.

Although production demands for the new 'Bay' model resulted in the Hanover factory being overwhelmed, with the result that Emden took over manufacture of Kombis, Microbuses and Microbus Ls bound for the United States, uncertain times lay ahead. The new Director General, Kurt Lotz, appeared determined to rid himself of the Beetle but lacked the expertise to produce an acceptable replacement. After four years Lotz was replaced by an old Volkswagen hand, Rudolph Leiding. He pushed through drastic changes, the result of which was that of all the old air-cooled models only the Bay had any long-term prospects.

The problems caused by recurrent oil crises, Middle East wars, world recession and, above all, a bank balance heavily in the red brought about Leiding's early retirement. In February 1975 Volkswagen appointed its fourth Director General in less than ten years, Toni Schmücker. One of his first acts was to confirm that a third-generation Transporter would have a rear-mounted air-cooled engine! The second-generation Transporter and its eventual successor had weathered the storm, even though by the mid 1970s production at Emden had ceased as cheaper Japanese imports had started to make inroads into Volkswagen's traditional territory, including the all-important and lucrative American market.

Based on the same principles as its predecessor, incorporating a sturdy frame of two full-length longitudinal members, braced with robust

Oppostie:
The setting is suitably prestigious and the theme is one that had been used in the days of the first-generation Microbus Deluxe. Somehow the second-generation top of the range model did not share the same level of exclusiveness as its predecessor.

The panoramic windscreen of the new Transporter launched in the summer of 1967 led to its being known by enthusiasts as the 'Bay'.

cross-members and reinforced outriggers, carefully incorporated into the main body structure, the second-generation model was quickly nicknamed the 'Bay' owing to its panoramic front windscreen. Gone were the split panes of old, replaced by a new single screen offering 27 per cent more glass than previously.

Fewer but much larger side windows for the Kombi and Microbuses made a healthy contribution to the updated look, while at its front the Bay retained a good deal of its predecessor's happy appearance. Below the windscreen a prominent grille formed a crucial part of the vehicle's fresh-air ventilation system, while large rectangular indicators placed above the bumper were prominent enough for other drivers to see. The sturdy bumper was of a wrap-around nature and cleverly incorporated a rubber-covered cab step at either end. Changes at the vehicle's rear were not instantly noticeable, making it easy for the less experienced to mistake an early second-generation

The Microbus Deluxe in second-generation guise incorporated more chrome and other brightwork than the less expensive Microbus but nevertheless lacked the individuality of its split-screen predecessor.

example for one of the later split-windscreen Transporters. The side elevation of all the second-generation models benefited from a sliding door, an extra-cost option in the latter years of first-generation production.

At 4,420 mm, the new Transporter was some 140 mm longer than its predecessor, although the wheelbase of 2,400 mm was identical to that of the older vehicle, the difference being accounted for by increased overhangs at both the front and rear of the new example. The second-generation Transporter stood some 50 mm taller than its forerunner, although the difference in width amounted to only 15 mm. Usable interior space went up from 4.8 to 5.0 cubic metres, an important consideration for Camper conversion manufacturers and firms wishing to cram a Delivery Van to its gills. More space was available owing primarily to a floor lower in comparison to that of the old model, something made possible due to the incorporation of a double-joint rear axle with semi-trailing arms. This device replaced the earlier bulky swinging axle arrangement. Ferdinand Porsche's patented independent torsion-bar system remained an important feature of the new Transporter's composition, the tubes being attached as an integral part of the chassis, making for a far sturdier overall arrangement. Although improved road-holding was largely a result of an increase in track, which now stood at 1,426 mm at the front and 1,384 mm at the rear, the revised set-up was undoubtedly a contributory factor.

On the minus side, the new model weighed about 105 kg more than its predecessor. Although the 1500 engine that had powered the first-generation Transporter in its final years of production had been widely praised, there was still a feeling that the first-generation model was in danger of lagging behind the competition in terms of power. Volkswagen's only option with

This year, as usual, we've changed the Volkswagen Station Wagon.

Below left:
Volkswagen's approach to the new model was somewhat unusual – almost implying an upgrade rather than a brand-new vehicle.

The VW Kombi
It has a 177 cu. ft. load compartment or seats for 2 to 8 people.

Below:
This image of the Kombi version of the Bay shows off an early model's features: indicators close to the bumpers, large VW roundel, external cab step-ups formed from an elongation of the bumper.

Volkswagen's press office was quick to ensure that images were available that included the full second-generation model line-up, but in this photograph the High-Top Delivery Van is absent.

the new and heavier model therefore had to be to increase engine power once more. The new 1,584cc engine developed a maximum of 47 PS at 4,000 rpm. Bore and stroke stood at 85.5 mm by 69.0 mm and the compression ratio at 7.7:1. Of most significance was the further increase in torque to a maximum of 103 Nm at 2,200 rpm. Volkswagen's ever conservative top speed of 105 km/h was of less interest to purchasers than the claims made in sales literature that quicker acceleration through the gears was possible, as was safer overtaking.

Unlike in the days of the initial launch in late 1949 and the spring of 1950, when additions to the range were subsequently rolled out on a progressive basis, the full list of new Transporter options had to be available from the start. With the passing of the years, the Kombi, with its lack of a full roof-panel trim, and absence of any form of trim panelling in all but the cab area, began to look increasingly primitive, although it still provided an ideal base from which numerous Camper manufacturers could work. The always somewhat ungainly High Top Delivery Van lost its all-metal structure in favour of a moulded glass-fibre roof, which to the aesthetically sensitive looked like an upturned bath or an enormous elongated jelly mould.

Designated the Clipper at launch, the Microbus was described by Volkswagen's United Kingdom press office as an 'estate car', while it was also noted that a Camper version was on offer.

However, of all the options it was the top of the range people-carrier that suffered the greatest. No longer known as the Microbus Deluxe, this vehicle and its lesser sibling, previously the Microbus, were now referred to as the Clipper L and Clipper respectively, Volkswagen paying scant regard to others' use of this name. The British Overseas Airways Corporation (BOAC) had been running a series of flights to North America under the Clipper Class brand for some years and not unreasonably objected to Volkswagen's use of the name. A short but acrimonious battle followed, but Volkswagen soon gave in, quickly renaming its people-carriers in the time-honoured style.

Unfortunately, the Microbus L also suffered a loss of identity. No longer did the vehicle boast more windows than the rest, while its traditional two-tone look was not instantly apparent, as only the roof panel benefited from a contrasting shade of paint. The vehicle did have chromed hubcaps and brightwork surrounds to each window, while it also sported a chromed border to the frontal air-intake grille, a bright strip along the swage lines under the side windows, a chrome VW roundel on its front, and rubber trims on both the front and back bumpers, but even so it no longer stood out from the crowd as it had done previously. To add insult to injury, by April 1968 its previously exclusive metal sunroof became an option on other passenger-carrying models.

Below left:
Volkswagen was justifiably proud of the new Transporter's dashboard, which demonstrated features that could only be described as thoroughly modern in 1968.

Below:
From August 1971 the size of the rear lights was upgraded. A heated rear window was a possibility, as was a metal sunroof on models other than a Microbus Deluxe.

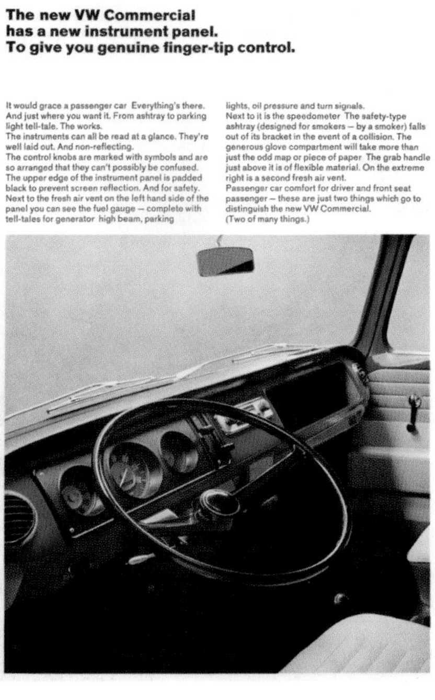

The new VW Commercial
has a new instrument panel.
To give you genuine finger-tip control.
It would grace a passenger car Everything's there. And just where you want it. From ashtray to parking light tell-tale. The works.
The instruments can all be read at a glance. They're well laid out. And non-reflecting.
The control knobs are marked with symbols and are so arranged that they can't possibly be confused.
The upper edge of the instrument panel is padded black to prevent screen reflection. And for safety.
Next to the fresh air vent on the left hand side of the panel you can see the fuel gauge – complete with tell-tales for generator high beam, parking lights, oil pressure and turn signals.
Next to it is the speedometer The safety-type ashtray (designed for smokers – by a smoker) falls out of its bracket in the event of a collision. The generous glove compartment will take more than just the odd map or piece of paper The grab handle just above it is of flexible material. On the extreme right is a second fresh air vent.
Passenger car comfort for driver and front seat passenger – these are just two things which go to distinguish the new VW Commercial.
(Two of many things.)

American sales brochures for second-generation Transporters were presented very much in the same style as those produced in the final years of first-generation manufacture. The vehicle depicted is a Microbus L.

The big difference between a Volkswagen Station Wagon and other station wagons is the box ours comes in.
Other wagons are basically sedans. With extra carrying space tagged onto the back end.
Ours is basically a big carrying space. With a VW added in. (Not the whole thing, of course. Just our air-cooled engine, a solid steel bottom, 4-wheel independent suspension. And some of the other things that make our cars such good little cars.)
True, a sedan-like wagon is sleeker looking than a box. And inside, our box does have a way of looking frighteningly empty —when it's empty.
Inside, however, most of those sleek jobs can carry only about half what our box can carry. So they start looking uncomfortably full while ours is still about half empty.
Once you understand these basics, you begin to see the Volkswagen Station Wagon for what it really is. Not the wagon that looks best. But the one that gets full last.
That's the beauty of it.
It's the box that makes it the car it is.

SALES STATISTICS

Demand for the new Transporter was particularly strong in the initial period of production. In 1968, the first full year of manufacture, 253,919 examples were built worldwide, a figure well in excess of the best year for the earlier model. More was to follow, until production peaked in 1972, when 294,932 Transporters of varying specifications were built. Although recession and many other factors brought upward sales figures to an abrupt halt in 1973, nevertheless even in 1978, its last full year of manufacture, nearly 207,000 examples rolled off assembly lines the world over.

UPDATING THE PRODUCT

Although Nordhoff was no longer present, his strategy of continual improvement was maintained, at least as far as the Transporter was concerned, throughout its years in production. Whether or not this state of

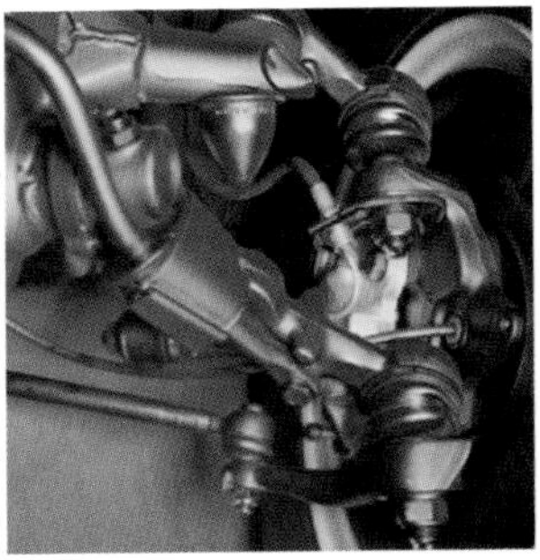

affairs was entirely voluntary, or the result of pressures from rival manufacturers, will remain a matter of debate, although the power game that ensued might suggest the latter.

In August 1970 the 1600 engine's cylinder heads were modified, the result being two inlet ports instead of one. Resultant easier breathing created the bonus of an increase in maximum power, up from 47 PS to 50 PS achieved at 4,000 rpm. This boost, however moderate, appeared to prompt the fitting of front discs, a move that not only improved stopping power considerably but also made the Transporter as efficient in this department as any of its rivals. The design of the vehicle's wheels was changed at the same time, becoming wider and featuring a series of more effective round ventilation holes. The traditional and elegant domed hubcap was replaced by a flat version, while the new wheels were sprayed with silver rather than the previous white paint.

In August 1971 a larger engine was introduced to run alongside the 1600 in Europe and to replace it in the United States. The 'new' engine had originally seen service in Volkswagen's largest air-cooled car, the ill-fated 411, which had been introduced some six months after Nordhoff's death.

Disc brakes made their debut in August 1970 at a point when the 1600 engine was upgraded to a rating of 50 PS. Twelve months later the first suitcase engine, the 1700, arrived.

This Microbus Deluxe dates from the 1972 model year. Note the flat hubcaps, the wheels with circular ventilation holes, the outline of a larger rear light cluster, and the early-style step-up.

The 1973 model-year Transporter received something of a makeover. Note the sturdier bumpers, the disappearance of the external step-up, and the new frontal design with the indicators adjacent to the air-intake grille.

Described by enthusiasts as the suitcase design, the cooling fan had been moved from the top of the engine and was now fitted on the nose of the crankshaft, making it more compact in both appearance and reality. Although it was originally produced in this way to fit neatly into the confines of the design of the 411, most experts would agree that, with a fan enclosed within an aluminium alloy housing planned to conduct air over the engine in a channelled arrangement of ducts, more efficient cooling was achieved. With a bore and stroke of 90 mm by 60 mm, the 1,679cc engine developed 66 PS at 4,800 rpm. Best of all though, for all those who had demanded twin carburettors before, the 1700 engine sported just such a feature.

Having fallen victim to the larger-engine syndrome once, Volkswagen succumbed twice more in the remaining years of second-generation Transporter production. An 1800 engine, again a by-product of the 411/412

In its final years of production, the second-generation Microbus L had the bright trim strips positioned to align with the cab and sliding-door handles.

series, was offered as a replacement for the 1700 with effect from August 1973. Although this 1,795cc engine produced only 2 PS more than the 1700 and little in the way of an increase in top speed, the gain in torque was significant. In August 1975 the 1600 engine was joined by a 2.0-litre unit, this time borrowed from the VW Porsche 914. With 70 PS achieved at 4,200 rpm and maximum torque of 143 Nm at 2,800 rpm at its disposal, competitive hill-climbing abilities and the capability to keep up with the rest of the pack, the Volkswagen was finally at least equal to its main competitors. Fuel consumption, however, was another matter.

Towards the end of second-generation Transporter production, European brochures no longer featured eye-catching imagery. This American publication, although clearly carefully posed, offers a glimpse of 1970s lifestyles.

All examples bound for the United States and fitted with either an 1800 or a 2-litre engine were also equipped with Bosch Jetronic fuel injection to meet the requirements of state legislation. Also, and primarily for the benefit of the American market, a three-speed automatic was introduced in the summer of 1972.

Finally, one major bodywork overhaul was of particular significance. Although the rear light clusters had been greatly enlarged on all models in August 1971, it was twelve months later when the main update took place. From this point all Transporters were fitted with sturdier U-section bumpers, very much in the style of those allocated to most Beetles since the summer of 1967. Additionally, the new front bumper lacked the wrap-arounds necessary to create a cab step up, this now being created within the body of the vehicle. The Transporter's frontal appearance was further amended through the relocation of the indicators to positions at either end of the air-intake grille, while the once prominent VW roundel was both reduced in size and positioned lower on the front panel.

Late 1970s tastes in colour are not necessarily those of the twenty-first century. The unusual combination depicted features Mexico Beige over Sage Green.

...you'll appreciate
your Devon
every day.
The Eurovettes and Devonettes

THE CAMPER REVOLUTION

TO ALL BUT the experts, an elderly VW Microbus and a Camper Van are one and the same thing. However, until the early years of the twenty-first century, Volkswagen had never itself manufactured a Camper version of its much vaunted Transporter range. Perhaps the business has only itself to blame for this widespread misconception, and particularly so in North America. The truth behind the legend is that the North Rhine-based caravan and trailer manufacturing company of Westfalia saw the near endless possibilities behind the Kombi and, in liaison with Volkswagen throughout, set about producing a series of camping kits and conversions that by the end of the 1950s had become firmly established in the market place.

In Britain others were reasonably quick to adopt the camping idea, from pioneers such as the now relatively unknown Peter Pitt, later Canterbury Pitt, and the aptly branded Devon models, the brainchild of Sidmouth-based cabinet-makers J. P. White, to later entrants, including the well-known name of Dormobile and the once popular Danbury. Despite, for example, Devon's reassurances that its products were fully approved by Volkswagen, it was only during the 1970s that Volkswagen of Great Britain actively promoted such products and then only when Devon had added an import to its books, the aptly named Continental – in reality a fully fledged Westfalia model.

In the United States and Canada the story was somewhat different. By the late 1950s promotional material made open reference to 'The Volkswagen Camper with Westfalia De Luxe equipment', while specific sales brochures were produced proclaiming the merits of such vehicles. Such was the demand for Westfalia's product that Volkswagen of America had little option but to augment stocks with a kit that might be fitted at home by a proficient DIY enthusiast, or, for the less adept, could be installed by a dealer on either a new or used Splitty. Such was the similarity of the kits to the genuine Westfalia item that some wit soon coined the term 'Westfakia' to describe the American-made items. When VW Canada launched the Canadiana in 1963, a rather basic kit costing $395, the spell was cast for the foreseeable future, while a new word, 'Campmobile', entered the motoring dictionary.

Opposite:
This image from a 1976 Devon brochure goes a long way to explain why many think of all Transporters as Campers. The vehicles that lack a sunroof could easily be straightforward Kombis or Microbuses.

Peter Pitt was a pioneer of the motorised caravan movement in Britain. The sales literature produced here dates from the last years of the 1950s.

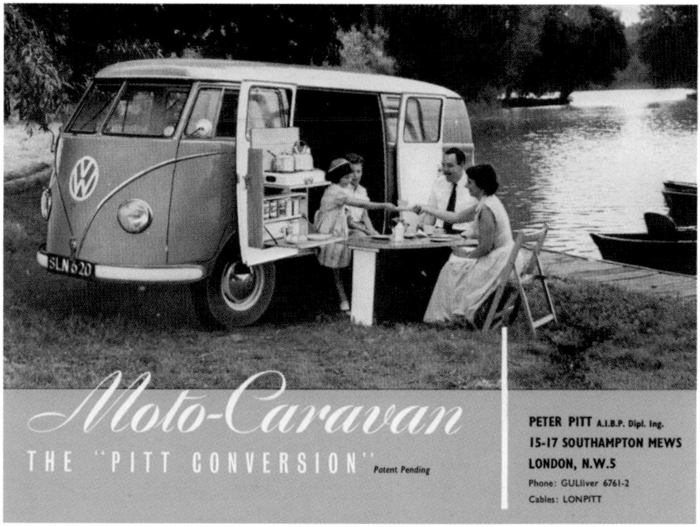

Initially devised to describe the locally manufactured kits, the word became synonymous with any form of Camper in North America. Before long, American sales literature referred to the people-carrying models as

Although Essex-based Danbury produced its first Camper conversion in 1964, it was during the era of the Bay that the firm became well known, even acquiring status as an officially approved converter.

Top left:
Dormobile had been producing Campers for a number of years before adding Volkswagens to its portfolio in 1961. This tiny brochure was carefully crafted to look like a passport – 'Dormobile, the Passport to New Frontiers'.

Top right:
Based in London, European Cars carried out its first conversion on a VW Microbus in 1958. It was branded the 'Slumberwagen', but low sales resulted in production ceasing in 1965.

Vanagons, while adjacent text discussed the Campmobile. Nor did the story end there, as other VW factories and dealers saw the merits in such a name.

Volkswagen in Australia initially endeavoured to import sufficient Westfalia models to meet demand, but, when the Clayton factory charged with assembling CKD kits from Germany was turned over to full manufacture, shortages of Campers inevitably led to home-built

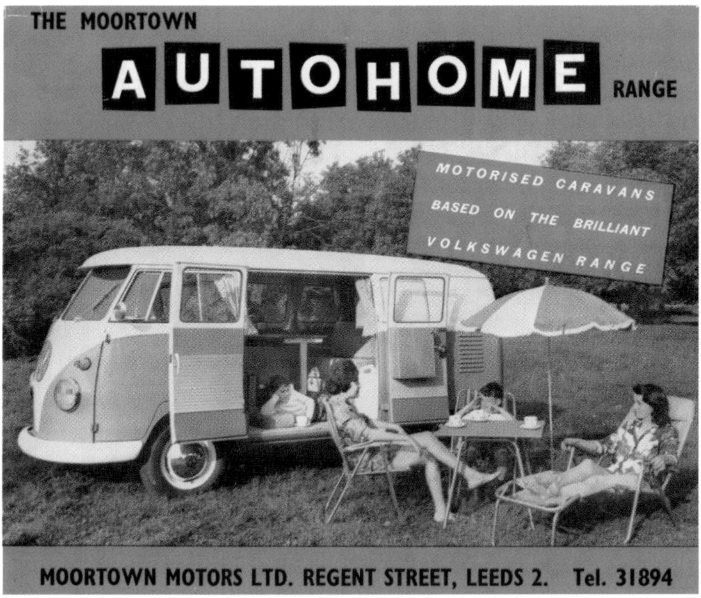

Moortown Motors, a Leeds-based Volkswagen distributor, contracted a local cabinet-making firm of repute to produce its first 'Moortown Caravan Conversion' in 1958, which was soon branded as the Autohome. Production ceased in the mid 1960s.

The cult of the Campmobile developed during the 1960s as Volkswagen of America supplied or even fitted camping kits, as demand for Westfalia's products outstripped supply.

Volkswagen of America's promotional literature for its camping kits carried all the style and panache evident for the rest of the range at this time. This illustration dates from 1962.

Campmobiles that bore a remarkable similarity to the original. Later, at roughly the point when the first-generation Transporter was succeeded by the second, CKD assembly was re-established in Australia. The time appeared right to hand over Camper manufacture to an Australian company with sufficient expertise to handle quality conversions. The result was that E. Sopru & Company produced a variety of models of Campmobile of varying specification and price throughout the 1970s, although their remit also extended to preparing Dormobiles under licence.

MADE IN CANADA
buy this kit (for only $395.00)*
install it yourself
and you have your cottage on wheels

Above left:
The Canadiana was Volkswagen of Canada's answer to the availability dilemma caused by a lack of Westfalia models. It could be fitted to either a 'Window Van or Delivery Van'.

Above:
VW Australia built its own Campers of a similar style to those produced by Westfalia in the 1960s. However, in 1968 E. Sopru was commissioned to convert 'completely knocked-down' kits into Campmobiles.

THE WESTFALIA STORY

Westfalia's working relationship with Volkswagen emerged in 1951 when it was approached by an American officer based in Germany to build an interior for a VW Kombi, a vehicle based very much on the design of caravans in years gone by. Having accomplished this task, Westfalia built several more, and one such Camper was exhibited at the Frankfurt Motor Show of 1952. A second theme surfaced in 1953 when Westfalia utilised the Kombi's greatest attribute, its flexibility, in recognition of the fact that only the minority could afford to operate one vehicle during the week and a second at weekends. The result was the Camping Box – literally a versatile, multi-purpose piece of furniture that could be dropped into a Kombi on a Saturday, only to be removed again on a Monday morning, when the vehicle was required to carry the products of a person's trade.

As the 1950s progressed, initially sluggish sales accelerated, with the majority of production being destined for the United States market. In 1958 Westfalia went as far as to introduce an official Camper assembly line, while at around the same time the vehicles produced were allocated special model (*Sonderausführungen*) status. Hence, SO1 was the code for a mobile shop and also produced for Volkswagen by Westfalia, and the SO22 was the Camping Box, at least between 1958 and 1962, while the SO23 was the fully fledged and fitted-out Camper.

Right:
During the late 1950s Volkswagen began to issue brochures specific to a Camper with Westfalia Deluxe equipment. Artwork gave way to photography, at least on the covers. Both these images feature vehicles that bore the designation SO23 in Europe.

Below:
Carefully posed shots were a hallmark of the brochure produced to promote sales of the SO35, a conversion that was introduced in 1961. A toy dog, sand acquired from the local builder's merchant, a studio backdrop and strategically placed shrubbery all add up to a brochure that is highly collectable for its cheesy nature!

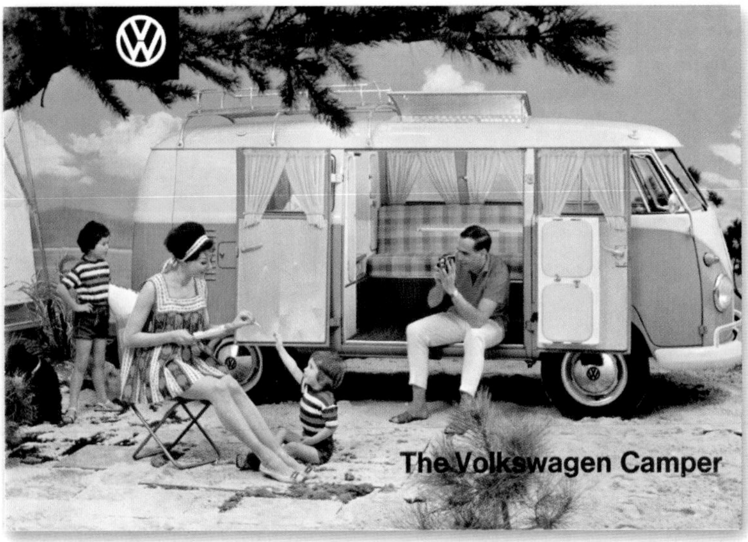

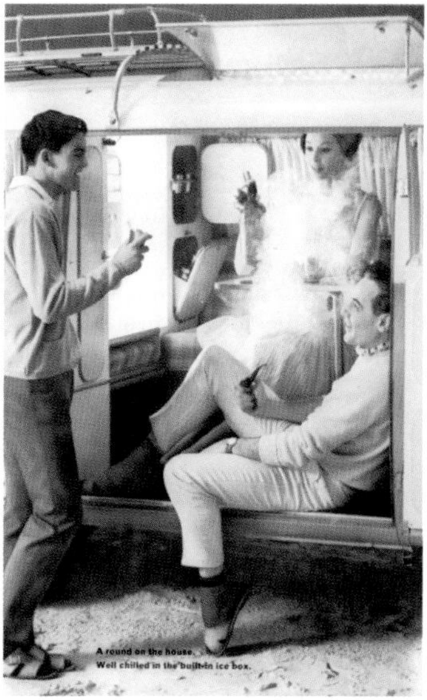

Cooking in a party dress and heels and blotting out the background with pipe smoke might appear amusing to us now, but Volkswagen cleverly recognised people's aspirations in the early 1960s.

To describe the intricacies of each SO variation would require a volume in its own right, so it must suffice to say that, while layouts changed with experience, each contained the basics of plentiful storage cupboards including a wardrobe, a collapsible table for dining and other purposes, a system whereby cushion seating could be rearranged to form a reasonably comfortable bed, and a rudimentary cooker. Deluxe offerings invariably added a cool-box unit, while washing facilities including water storage were

In the era of the second-generation Transporter an array of US brochures depicted what lucky Campmobile owners might come to expect as the norm. This image shows the new front-hinged elevating roof option.

From 1969 to 1971 each Westfalia conversion was given the name of a major European city in addition to its SO code. Externally, each model appeared very similar.

catered for. Peripheral items such as hammocks and awnings might well be available, but invariably at extra cost.

The wonderful space-creating device of an elevating roof originated as nothing more than a small fling-back panel, while a roof rack was commonplace. By 1965 the 'submarine hatch', as wits described it, had been replaced by two options: Westfalia's diminutive canvas-sided pop-top; or a full-length Martin Walter Dormobile elevating roof. Whereas it would have

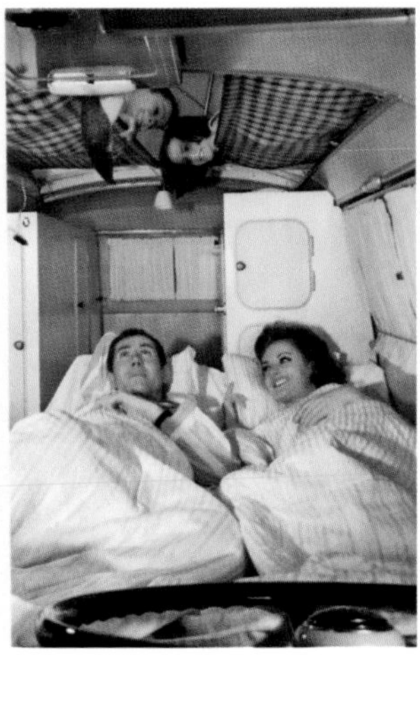

Images for a brochure produced in 1964 not only indicate the quality of the fittings of a Westfalia camper but also illustrate the formality of the era, even when on holiday.

Westfalia models produced after September 1973 featured a new style of elevating roof that was hinged at the rear. From 1975 Helsinki and Berlin became the key options, although the American Campmobile varied slightly.

been impossible for one motor manufacturer to utilise panels or parts from another, the situation was very different in the Camper business.

With the arrival of the new generation of Transporters in the summer of 1967, Westfalia's sales started to multiply out of all proportion. On 8 March 1968 the 30,000th Camper to be produced rolled off the assembly line and, soon after, the company was producing eighty conversions per day. In 1971 the 100,000th Camper was produced, while, to emphasise the importance of the American market, of the 22,500 units produced more than 19,000 were destined for the United States. In recognition of this, Westfalia had started to produce Campers specifically aimed at the American market, the first such being based on the Delivery Van rather than the Kombi. Typical of the early to mid second-generation Transporter era of conversions is the list of options

While Volkswagen relied on simple line drawings to illustrate the layouts and facilities of Westfalia's products, they preferred to use carefully posed photography to sell the camping lifestyle.

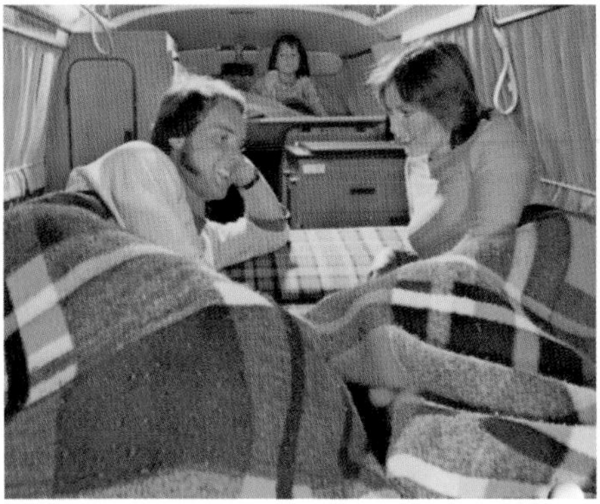

These two interior shots promote the Westfalia Helsinki conversion on the second-generation Transporter.

for 1972, which totalled six in number. While the Luxembourg, Helsinki and Madrid were clearly aimed at European takers, the Los Angeles, Houston and Miami, as their names indicate, were destined for American consumption.

Unfortunately, the oil crisis of 1973 brought a drop in American sales of some 35 per cent and while there was a degree of market recovery, particularly following the introduction of a further selection of models, the heady days were over.

Westfalia developed the Continental in 1972, a model specifically for countries where right-hand drive prevailed. The complexities of the market and Volkswagen's strategy resulted in this model being listed as part of the Devon range.

Dating from 1958, this very early example of a Devon brochure features the recently launched Caravette. Based on the Microbus, the high-quality conversion incorporated hand-polished light oak.

DEVON

When in 1957 a Sidmouth-based firm of cabinet-makers entered a loose partnership with the VW dealers Lisburne Garages, the best-known British brand name in the field of VW Campers was born. J. P. White employed

Although not in the league of Volkswagen's own printed material by the early 1960s Devon's brochures featured a colour image on the cover which aimed to convey the outdoor lifestyle a Caravette owner could enjoy.

skilled cabinet-makers, and the conversions they produced featured craftsmanship of unequalled merit. In 1960 they were able to boast of solid oak fittings, electric and gas lighting, Formica surfaces, a full set of crockery for four people, an 'Easicool' food-storage cabinet, and an 18-litre water container.

Brand names came and went with amazing alacrity: Devonette and Torvette were two of the names allocated to no-frills models; Caravette and later Eurovette and Moonraker were names typical of the more luxurious

Devon's brochure image dating from late 1964: by this time the Caravette conversion could be ordered on the Microbus or Microbus Deluxe, while the lower-priced Devonette was available on a Kombi or Microbus.

A hardworking Devon motor caravan
earns its holidays in the sun

Devon.
The motor caravan
that's as good as a VW.

By the end of first-generation production, Devon was openly emphasising the dual role that the Caravette and lowlier Torvette could play. Note how the cooker could be swung round from its normal position.

As the 1970s progressed, Devon's literature became increasingly sophisticated, while the company endeavoured to produce two kinds of conversion: a multi-purpose vehicle, and a high-specification Camper.

Following the arrival of the new Transporter, Devon extended its offer, adding a top of the range model, which they called the Eurovette. Like the Caravette, this model was based on the Clipper or Microbus.

end of the market. For example, the range in 1966 consisted of the Caravette and Torvette, the former available as a conversion on either the Microbus or, at considerably more cost, the Microbus Deluxe. The Caravette Spaceway (to complicate matters further) was an option based on the Microbus but featuring access from the cab to the rear of the vehicle, rather than the traditional bulkhead approach. The Torvette, on the other hand, was exclusive to the Kombi, lacked some of the trimmings accorded to the other models and could be distinguished by its single-colour exterior paint.

As the years passed, chipboard and other cost-cutting economy items regrettably made their almost inevitable appearance. By way of compensation, layouts became more elaborate and once undreamt-of mod cons appeared, while items such as the Devon double-top elevating roof were simple to operate thanks to devices such as gas struts.

While large segments of the respective first- and second-generation Transporter stories could have been allocated to detailed descriptions of the various layouts offered by a myriad of craftsmen, this would have made for a dull read. Nevertheless, we have established that the Camper was not a Volkswagen-produced product, and the potted history of the Transporter given, together with copious images of Campers, should provide an encompassing picture.

The Devon Eurovette's interior was far from basic and offered decent accommodation for a family of four. The cushions were covered in reversible vinyl and 'Duracour' fabric.

THE ICONIC TRANSPORTER

If the ground-breaking, redoubtable, yet quirkily simple promotional campaign of the advertising agency Doyle Dane Bernbach genuinely generated countless additional sales in the 1960s to fill Volkswagen's coffers, then the Flower Power generation and a movement emanating from California inspired the Transporter's evolution to its current cult status.

The Transporter, particularly in Camper guise, is and has been the 'cool' transport choice of the Flower Power generation and the surfing community. On the eve of the celebrations for the Transporter's sixtieth anniversary, held in Hanover in the autumn of 2007, Stephan Schaller from Volkswagen Commercial Vehicles in Germany spoke of the vehicle invoking more emotions than any other. 'It is a real cult vehicle and has stood for fun, independence and travel as well as business success', he said. A key element to those festivities was Volkswagen's wish to celebrate the Transporter's strong links with the music industry over the years, and to this end a band with its roots in the 1960s performed a concert harking back to the days of Flower Power, love, peace and rock 'n' roll.

The Camper, possibly the humble Delivery Van and even the Kombi leant themselves to either short or lengthy excursions in search of peace, love or conceivably political agitation; the Camper particularly catered for an outdoor lifestyle – of balmy evenings spent around a camp fire, guitars strumming, smoke curling from whatever substance those present chose to partake of. With avarice and materialism apparently far from the participants' minds, perhaps inevitably the attendant Transporter would be more than a few years old, in need of a lick of paint and possibly even life-lengthening patches. Pristine originality through costly restoration was far from the minds of such owners. Here was an opportunity to echo their unconventional dress and free-spirit appearance in their transport. Gaudily painted flowers and symbols of peace mingled with brightly coloured patterns, all executed with household paints and brushes.

Running parallel to such extravagances was a growing cult of customisation, a movement where factory originality was an anathema to

Opposite:
Find a stretch of coastline ideal for surfing and a Volkswagen Transporter won't be far away! With links dating back several decades, the cruising and surfing movement is now synonymous with VW Camper vans, preferably older examples!

Volkswagen's British Press Office circulated this image of a Flower Power generation Transporter to promote the sixtieth anniversary celebrations to be held at Hanover in 2007. (Courtesy Volkswagen UK)

owners. Principal among this faction was the 'Cal-look' Transporter, a concept initiated in California and still popular to this day. The look is epitomised by lowered suspension and possibly a narrowed front beam, a much more powerful and visually sparkly engine than Volkswagen's standard issue, aftermarket wheels such as EMPI five-spokes or Porsche-style Fuch replicas, and well-executed paint finishes in either appealing pastels or strident primary colours. A true Cal-look vehicle will lack any form of chrome or anodised trim and might feature the smoothing out of such items

This shot of a Westfalia interior taken in 2008 indicates how the Camper enthusiast might decide to retain some degrees of originality, whilst also introducing elements that suit his or her personal tastes.

as door handles. However, the so-called 'Resto-Cal' owner will have retained or possibly even have added to the brightwork. The interior of a Cal or Resto-Cal will undoubtedly have been heavily modified to suit both the tastes of the owner and the trends of the time. Costly leather or an exquisite imitation is commonplace; cleverly designed and accomplished craftsmanship in metal, wood and plastic is often apparent, while the inclusion of a state-of-the-art sound system is virtually guaranteed. Most Cal-look vehicles will have cost their owners many thousands of pounds to complete, not to mention the countless man-hours required to effect the transformation.

The Cal-look and other associated movements encompass a particular kind of lifestyle just as the Flower Power Transporters have done over the years. Such vehicles are most regularly associated with the sea, sand and, above all, surf. Regular rallies, such as Britain's 'Run to the Sun', held each year in Cornwall, have gathered pace, with 'cruising' forming an essential ingredient of the activities.

A more recent development has been the emergence of the 'rat-look' Transporter. These range from tired old vehicles that have been put on the road without any attempt to restore the bodywork and, if rumour is to be believed, with little effort mechanically over and above the requirements of the annual 'MOT' (Ministry of Transport test) in Britain, to Transporters that have been deliberately aged. Prime targets for such treatment are vehicles that have spent many years in dry and sunny climes, where the effect of prolonged exposure to sunlight has removed or at least bleached a large percentage of the paint. Treated with either the permanence of a clear lacquer, or coated with less enduring wax, such Transporters are characterised by dull, flat paint and patches of orange or brown surface rust. Panel vans and Pick-ups so presented might well feature evidence of

Take an original but tired Transporter and deliberately age the paintwork, add aftermarket wheels, rare and collectable accessories, and then lower the vehicle. This is the 'rat look'!

When such respected institutions as the BBC use the ubiquitous Transporter for some of their regional broadcasting, it is quickly appreciated just what a cult vehicle the humble bus has become. This example has even been personalised!

apparently long-ago-applied signwriting, whereas this has in fact been added in yet another attempt to age the vehicle. Ground-scraping lowered suspension, deliberately aged period accessories – ranging from roof racks to air-scoops – are also traits of the rat-look vehicle. Modified engines, if they have been fitted, are not immaculately shiny, while the average rat-look interior is likely to extend the feeling of a well-worn, well-used vehicle.

However much owners of pristine vehicles presented exactly as they left the factory might splutter with indignation at the antics of the custom fraternity, without them the Transporter enthusiast scene would be much smaller, while the imagination of the general public would be less likely to be captivated by the ubiquitous 'Bus'. Europe's largest Transporter gathering, the Vanfest at Malvern, attracting well over ten thousand people each year, is representative of the enthusiast movement in that well over 60 per cent of the vehicles in attendance will not be presented in the same way as they left Hanover back in the 1980s or earlier.

Today the owners of older Transporters include famous personalities such as actors and television chefs, at least one of whom displays genuine enthusiasm for the marque. The BBC even holds a second-generation Transporter or two on its inventory. Weddings and funerals are catered for: brides can hire a specially trimmed Camper for their big day, while a business offering Transporter hearses has emerged. Companies producing giftware for holidaymakers are virtually guaranteed to include representations of Transporters in any retro range they offer. From coasters to key-rings, toast-racks to egg-cups, candle holders to countless coffee mugs, the Transporter holds sway. Television commercials are littered with Transporters linked to the most unrelated of products, film heroes dive past the latest in luxury metal to climb aboard Transporters capable of phantasmagorical feats, while professional photographers know that the inclusion of a Transporter in a shot is more likely to sell the image.

CONCLUSION

One of Tony Schmücker's first acts after his appointment as Volkswagen's Director General was to confirm that the third generation of Transporters would have their engines at the rear and be air-cooled in time-honoured fashion. That was in 1975, and at a point when water-cooled technology was just starting to pay dividends for Volkswagen. For a little under three years after its launch in August 1979, the third-generation Transporter was indeed an air-cooled vehicle, sporting both a 2.0-litre and a grossly underpowered suitcase-style 1600 engine. But with the expensive and exclusive development of a water-cooled 'boxer' engine (with cylinders horizontally opposed) for the Transporter, closely after the reworked Golf diesel engine, the end was in sight for the classic Microbus and Camper.

The VW Camper and Microbus story continued throughout the 1980s, the third-generation model, nicknamed the 'Wedge', taking on the mantle previously held by its predecessors.

Nevertheless, although not yet in the same league as its predecessors, the third-generation Transporter, sometimes known as the T3 or even the T25, but nicknamed the 'Wedge' by enthusiasts because of its slab-like appearance, has attracted its own band of followers, particularly when it comes to Camping conversions. The inevitable result has been that prices for good examples have started to rise. Noticeably more roomy than the second-generation model, it dates from an age when modern luxuries were starting to filter down to the common man, and it is likely that at some point an additional chapter will be required to complete the story of Volkswagen's classic Microbuses and Campers. Until that point arrives, a parting thought has to be that Westfalia's best-selling Camper in the eleven years of the third generation was the Joker. Could this be more apt?

INDEX

Page numbers in italic refer to illustrations